WILLIAM T. SHERMAN

David C. King

BLACKBIRCH PRESS

THOMSON
★
GALE

Detroit • New York • San Diego • San Francisco
Boston • New Haven, Conn. • Waterville, Maine
London • Munich

Published by Blackbirch Press
10911 Technology Place
San Diego, CA 92127
Web site: http://www.galegroup.com/blackbirch
e-mail: customerservice@galegroup.com

© 2002 by Blackbirch Press,
an imprint of The Gale Group

Printed in China

10 9 8 7 6 5 4 3 2 1

Photo credits:
Cover, back cover, pages 19, 35, 42, 46-47, 48, 50-51, 53, 57, 60-61, 62-63,
81, 84, 85, 90, 93 © North Wind Picture Archives; pages 9, 13, 16-17, 20,
36, 55, 56, 58, 59, 72, 79, 89, 96 © The Library of Congress; pages 10, 14,
24, 26, 30, 37, 40 © National Portrait Gallery; pages 12, 18, 23, 34, 45, 59,
60, 77, 85 © Dover Publications; pages 28-29, 31, 40, 66, 71 © National
Archives; page 44 © National Geographic Society; page 74 © CORBIS; page
98 © King Visual Technology

Library of Congress Cataloging-in-Publication Data
King, David C.,
William T. Sherman/ by David C. King.
        p. cm. — (The Civil War)
Includes index.
Summary: Discusses the life and career of William T. Sherman,
Confederate General
        ISBN 1-56711-563-2 (hardback : alk. paper)
1. Sherman, William T, 1820-1891—-Juvenile literature. [1. Generals—Union
Army—Biography—juvenile literature. 3. Union Army. Army—biography—
juvenile literature 4. United States-History-Civil War, 1961-1865—
Campaigns-juvenile literature [1. Sherman, William, 1820-1891-Juvenile
literature. 2. Generals Generals 3. Union Army—4 United States-History—
Civil War, 1861-1865.1. Title. II. Civil War (Blackbirch Press)
E467.1155 S47 2002
97307'3'092-dc   2002002480

CONTENTS

PREFACE: THE CIVIL WAR

Nearly 150 years after the final shots were fired, the Civil War remains one of the key events in U. S. history. The enormous loss of life alone makes it tragically unique: More Americans died in Civil War battles than in all other American wars combined. More Americans fell at the Battle of Gettysburg than during any battle in American military history. And, in one day at the Battle of Antietam, more Americans were killed and wounded than in any other day in American history.

Slaves did the backbreaking work on Southern plantations.

As tragic as the loss of life was, however, it is the principles over which the war was fought that make it uniquely American. Those beliefs—equality and freedom—are the foundation of American democracy, our basic rights. It was the bitter disagreement about the exact nature of those rights that drove our nation to its bloodiest war.

The disagreements grew in part from the differing economies of the North and South. The warm climate and wide-open areas of the Southern states were ideal for an economy based on agriculture. In the first half of the 19th century, the main cash crop was cotton, grown on large farms called plantations. Slaves, who were brought to the United States from Africa, were forced to do the backbreaking work of planting and harvesting cotton. They also provided the other labor necessary to keep plantations running. Slaves were bought and sold like property, and had been critical to the Southern economy since the first Africans came to America in 1619.

The suffering of African Americans under slavery is one of the great tragedies in American history. And the debate over whether the United States government had the right to forbid slavery—in both Southern states and in new territories—was a dispute that overshadowed the first 80 years of our history.

For many Northerners, the question of slavery was one of morality and not economics. Because the Northern economy was based on manufacturing rather than agriculture, there was little need for slave labor. The primary economic need of Northern states was a protective tax known as a tariff that would make imported goods more expensive than goods made in the North. Tariffs forced Southerners to buy Northern goods and made them economically dependent on the North, a fact that led to deep resentment among Southerners.

Economic control did not matter to the anti-slavery Northerners known as abolitionists. Their conflict with the South was over slavery. The idea that the federal government could outlaw slavery was perfectly reasonable. After all, abolitionists contended, our nation was founded on the idea that all people are created equal. How could slavery exist in such a country?

For the Southern states that joined the Confederacy, the freedom from unfair taxation and the right to make their

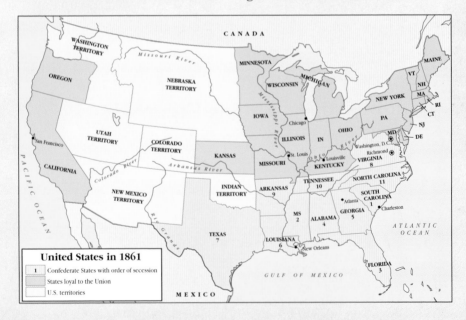

United States in 1861

1   Confederate States with order of secession
   States loyal to the Union
   U.S. territories

own decisions about slavery was as important a principle as equality. For most Southerners, the right of states to decide what is best for its citizens was the most important principle guaranteed in the Constitution.

The conflict over these principles generated sparks throughout the decades leading up to the Civil War. The importance of keeping an equal number of slave and free states in the Union became critical to Southern lawmakers in Congress in those years. In 1820, when Maine and Missouri sought admission to the Union, the question was settled by the Missouri Compromise: Maine was admitted as a free state, Missouri as a slave state, thus maintaining a balance in Congress. The compromise stated that all future territories north of the southern boundary of Missouri would enter the Union as free states, those south of it would be slave states.

In 1854, however, the Kansas-Nebraska Act set the stage for the Civil War. That act repealed the Missouri Compromise and by declaring that the question of slavery should be decided by residents of the territory, set off a rush of pro- and anti-slavery settlers to the new land. Violence between the two sides began almost immediately and soon "Bleeding Kansas" became a tragic chapter in our nation's story.

With Lincoln's election on an anti-slavery platform in 1860, the disagreement over the power of the federal government reached its breaking point. In early 1861, South Carolina became the first state to secede from the Union, followed by Mississippi, Florida, Alabama, Georgia, Louisiana, Virginia, Texas, North Carolina, Tennessee, and Arkansas. Those eleven states became the Confederate States of America. Confederate troops fired the first shots of the Civil War at Fort Sumter, South Carolina, on April 12, 1861. Those shots began a four-year war in which thousands of Americans—Northerners and Southerners—would give, in President Lincoln's words, "the last full measure of devotion."

OPPOSITE: The Confederate attack on Fort Sumter began the Civil War.

Introduction:
Enemies and Friends

★ ★ ★ ★ ★

On April 17, 1865, two generals met near a North Carolina hamlet called Durham's Station. The Union general, William Tecumseh Sherman, was there to accept the surrender of the Confederacy's Joseph Eggleston Johnston. Both knew the war was over—Robert E. Lee had surrendered to Ulysses S. Grant a week earlier.

The two men had been friends at West Point, but they became enemies in 1861 when Johnston resigned from the U.S. Army and accepted a commission in the Confederate Army. They had not seen each other since, but for a few months in 1864, they had engaged in a desperate conflict as Johnston tried to block Sherman's march on Atlanta. Johnston, with half as many men as Sherman, maneuvered brilliantly, kept his army intact, and prevented Sherman from taking Atlanta. Sherman had been just as brilliant. He had kept his three separate armies constantly on the move, which allowed him to steadily apply pressure on Johnston and edge closer to Atlanta.

Confederate President Jefferson Davis, however, became frustrated with Johnston's failure to launch a counterattack. In July 1864, he replaced Johnston with General John B. Hood.

While Johnston returned home, Sherman seized Atlanta and made his famous "March to the Sea"

On their "March to the Sea," Sherman and his men left Atlanta in ruins.

through Georgia. In February 1865, he turned north toward the Carolinas, with plans to connect with Grant near Richmond. Johnston was hastily called out of retirement and asked to patch together an army to stop Sherman. With only 30,000 men against Sherman's 85,000, however, Johnston could do little. On that April day, the only remaining question was what Sherman's terms of surrender would be.

Johnston anticipated harsh punishment. Instead, Sherman offered him lenient terms that Johnston willingly accepted, including food for his half-starved men. He later wrote to Sherman, "Your gesture of offering my men ten days' rations reconciles me to what I have previously regarded as the misfortune of my life, that of having you to encounter in the field." Sherman replied that he was "never so relieved as when you were removed from command outside Atlanta."

The two remained friends after the war, and they were united in death as well. Twenty-six years after the surrender, when Sherman died in February 1891, Johnston was at the funeral, standing hatless in a freezing rain. He contracted pneumonia and died a few days later.

Chapter 1

YEARS OF FAILURE

Tecumseh Sherman was born on February 8, 1820 in the town of Lancaster, Ohio, where his father, Charles, was a well-known judge. He was named after the great Shawnee warrior Tecumseh, but the priest who baptized him added the Christian name William (it was St. William's Day).

When William was nine years old, his father died. His mother soon married a family friend and powerful politician, Thomas Ewing. Ewing adopted young Sherman as "the brightest of the lot." With this new son, Ewing now had a family of eleven children.

OPPOSITE: Next to Ulysses S. Grant, William Tecumseh Sherman was the best-known Union general in the Civil War.

Sherman was named after Tecumseh, a Shawnee warrior.

"Cump," as young Sherman's friends called him, was tall and skinny, with a shock of red hair that he was often teased about (once he dyed it an ugly green). Despite the hair problem, he was very popular and regarded as a near-genius in school.

When William was sixteen, Thomas Ewing procured an appointment for him at West Point, the famous U.S. military academy on the Hudson River north of New York City. The Eastern relatives William saw on his way to the military academy regarded him as "an untamed animal just caught in the Far West." Even then, people had trouble understanding this scrawny youth. He was brilliant, everyone agreed, and he could take part in intelligent conversations better than most adults. But he was also headstrong, and preferred to go his own way, rather than to do what was expected of him.

Cadet Sherman was an outstanding student at West Point—strongest in engineering, geology, rhetoric, and philosophy. He was also outstanding

Sherman attended the U.S. Military Academy at West Point, pictured here in the early 1800s.

at collecting demerits for violating codes of discipline and dress. When he graduated in 1840, he should have ranked fourth in the class, but his demerits dropped him to sixth.

An Undistinguished Soldier

After being commissioned a lieutenant in the U.S. Army, Sherman was sent to Florida to fight the Seminole Indians. A courageous remnant of the

The Indian Removal Policy

In 1830, President Andrew Jackson yielded to the demands of white Americans and asked Congress to approve his Indian Removal policy. Nearly all of the tribes still living in the East were to be removed beyond the Mississippi. All of the good farmland east of the Mississippi had been taken, and land-hungry settlers had coveted the farms and hunting grounds of the tribes for years. Jackson had become convinced that Native Americans and European Americans could not live side by side.

Andrew Jackson

Throughout the 1830s, tribe after tribe was escorted across the Mississippi, with force if necessary. Five tribes had hoped to avoid this fate by adopting European ways. They established farms, built European-style houses, and allowed missionaries to start churches and schools.

But the five groups—known as the "Five Civilized Tribes"—found that these efforts did not protect them. They, too, were escorted to "Indian Territory," with hundreds dying of exposure and starvation. The Cherokee called this journey the "Trail of Tears."

One of the five tribes, the Seminole, fought for their freedom in Florida under the leadership of their great chief Osceola. The army captured Osceola, and most of the tribe was forced to join the westward trek, along with the Creek, Choctaw, and Chickasaw. A few hundred Seminoles escaped. Joined by a few Creek and some runaway slaves, they moved deep into the Everglades, where they remained into the 20th century. The U.S. government recognized their status as part of the Seminole nation in 1991.

tribe had moved deep into the Everglades, where they continued to resist the government's Indian Removal policy.

Sherman never saw any Seminoles but, according to his letters to his younger brother, John, he was "delighted" with the young ladies of St. Augustine. Sherman was transferred to Fort Moultrie, South Carolina, on a coastal island outside Charleston. A relative wrote that he was enjoying "horse-racing, picnicking, boating, fishing, swimming, and God knows what else."

After four years idling in South Carolina, Sherman was actually pleased when the nation declared war on Mexico in 1846. The trouble had been brewing for several years, since Texas had declared its independence from Mexico in 1836. When the United States annexed Texas in 1845, the two countries needed only a border incident to trigger the outbreak of fighting.

The U.S. government was moving aggressively into new territories because Americans were in an expansionist mood in the 1840s. People had developed the idea that it was America's Manifest Destiny (that is, its clear destiny, or fate) to expand its borders all the way to the Pacific Ocean. A good deal of Mexico's territory, including California, fit nicely into that vision.

For America's small army of professionals, and especially the officers trained at West Point, the war with Mexico provided an ideal occasion for

15

Unlike many Civil War generals, Sherman did not see action in the Mexican War. Instead, he served in an administrative post. Here, Mexican officers surrender to the United States.

practical experience. The Mexicans fought with great courage and determination, but they lacked the manpower and the weaponry to have any chance of winning. The conflict thus enabled many West Pointers to gain promotions and awards after they led their troops to victory.

While future generals such as Ulysses Grant and Robert E. Lee were gaining recognition and experience, however, the war was passing by William T. Sherman. He was trapped in an administrative job in California, where he remained until a territorial government was formed.

Back east again in 1850, he married Ellen Ewing, daughter of his adoptive father. Thomas Ewing was then serving in Washington as secretary of the interior. William and Ellen settled in St. Louis, where Sherman was stationed.

Still in the U.S. Army, Sherman became increasingly bored by commissary duties, which involved purchasing cattle in Missouri and Kansas. He felt a desire to "get somewhere"—to be a success. He had seen men making fortunes from the gold rush in California—not so much by making strikes in the gold fields, but by making shrewd investments in companies that filled the needs of miners for food, clothes, and shelter.

Thomas Ewing, Sherman's adoptive father, served as the first U.S. secretary of the interior.

Thousands of people seeking gold flocked to California in 1849.

In 1853, he decided it was time to leave the army and seek his fortune. He was now thirty-three years old and felt life was passing him by, especially when so many men he had known since West Point days had garnered glory in the Mexican War. He may have been motivated also by learning that his younger brother John, a

19

Sherman worked at a bank in San Francisco (shown here) in the mid-1850s.

lawyer, was going to run for election to the House of Representatives.

So Captain Sherman resigned from the army in September 1853. He joined a St. Louis bank, which sent him to San Francisco as its representative. He did well at first, mixing real estate with banking, but in 1857, California was struck by an economic recession and Sherman found himself $13,000 in debt. He also, he said, found himself "used up financially," and called himself "the Jonah of banking." In a letter to Ewing, he revealed his loss of self-confidence: "What I failed to accomplish, and the bad debts that now stare me in the face, must stand forever as a monument to my want of . . . sagacity."

Sherman paid most of the debts by selling his property. In 1858, he went back to Lancaster, Ohio, where Ewing owned a saltworks that Sherman could manage. It was humbling for a proud army officer, but with a wife and now three children, he was desperate for work. While Ellen was thrilled to be back home, Sherman felt humiliated—a feeling that was only aggravated by the fact that his younger brother was now in his second term in Congress.

Ewing's oldest son, Thomas Jr., asked Sherman to join him in a law firm in Kansas. He jumped at the opportunity and was easily accepted to the bar of the state "on the ground of general intelligence and reputation." Sherman, however, badly mangled his first case and, after that, had no clients. He had also tried speculating in corn, and he even encouraged his wife and father-in-law to invest. This was also a mistake. After Sherman and his family lost their investments, he carried the burden of shame with him and returned to Ohio.

Sherman may have had bad luck in business, but he always found people who were willing to help him. Two old Southern friends from his West Point days—Braxton Bragg and P. G. T. Beauregard—found a position for him as superintendent at a new

21

★

In March 1860,
Elizabeth Cady
Stanton presented
a case for women's
suffrage to the New
York State legislature.

★

school called the Louisiana State Seminary of Learning and Military Academy (now part of Louisiana State University).

For a few months, Sherman proved to be an excellent administrator and teacher. He enjoyed the work immensely and seemed to finally be coming into his own. And Ellen, who at first refused to join him and pestered him to come "home," eventually relented.

Before Ellen could make the move, however, leaders of several Southern states startled the nation by voting to secede from the Union. They did this after Republican Abraham Lincoln won the 1860 presidential election. Like millions of Americans, Sherman found his loyalties divided. He was not opposed to slavery and he had a deep fondness for the South, but he thought it was foolish to consider war. On Christmas Eve in 1860, he warned a Southern friend:

> This country will be drenched in blood... You people
> [Southerners] speak so lightly of war. You don't know
> what you are talking about. War is a terrible thing. You
> mistake, too, the people of the North. They are peaceable
> but earnest and will fight.... You are rushing into war
> with one of the most powerful, ingeniously mechanical
> and determined people on earth—right at your doors.
> You are bound to fail.

In the last analysis, Sherman's devotion to the Union made his decision easy. He resigned from the school, returned to St. Louis, and became president of the Fifth Street Railroad. Although Sherman did not have much confidence in Lincoln, he asked his brother, John Sherman— now a senator—to help him obtain a commission in the army from Lincoln's War Department. The president responded that no army officers were needed because the government planned to settle the North-South dispute through negotiation. Sherman, always nervous and high-strung, was upset. He was convinced that the government was being foolish, and determined that the next time he would wait until he got what he wanted.

Chapter 2

THE UNCERTAIN WARRIOR

$\mathbf{W}$hen Abraham Lincoln took the oath of office as president in March 1861, he faced a rebellion on the part of the states of the South. More states seceded in the following weeks until there were eleven states in the Confederacy. Virginia, one of the last states to secede, included some of the best military officers in the nation.

OPPOSITE: Jefferson Davis, former senator and army officer, was elected president of the Confederacy in 1861.

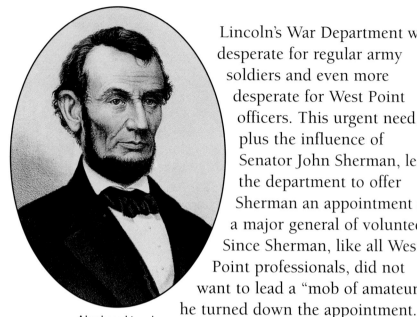

Lincoln's War Department was desperate for regular army soldiers and even more desperate for West Point officers. This urgent need, plus the influence of Senator John Sherman, led the department to offer Sherman an appointment as a major general of volunteers. Since Sherman, like all West Point professionals, did not want to lead a "mob of amateurs," he turned down the appointment.

Abraham Lincoln was elected president in 1860.

The War Department then offered him the post of quartermaster general, which he turned down, then assistant secretary of war. This, too, he rejected. He finally accepted a commission as colonel in the regular army.

As thousands of volunteers flooded into Washington, D.C., and established camps, the capital took on a military appearance. Dozens of regimental flags from all the Union states fluttered above clusters of tents while the recruits paraded in a colorful array of uniforms.

There were eager and willing men, but there was almost no military training. Colonel Sherman was upset to find that, instead of regular army, he was given a brigade of fresh recruits. "With Regulars I would have no doubts," he wrote to

Ellen, "but these volunteers are subject to stampedes."

The Union army's officers, including Sherman, were surprised in July when they were given orders to march against the Confederate army. Most of the Federal officers knew that their amateur army, with almost no training, was not much more than a gang with weapons. Lincoln's cabinet and military leaders saw the situation in simpler terms. In order to crush the rebellion, the Federals merely had to cross the Potomac River into Virginia, turn south, and march about 110 miles where they would capture Richmond, the capital of the Confederacy.

★

Jefferson Davis resigned from the U.S. Senate in 1861.

★

A Lesson in War at Bull Run

With bands playing and crowds shouting the battle cry, "Forward to Richmond!" about 30,000 Union troops marched toward Richmond. Carriages filled with picnickers and politicians followed along, hoping to catch a glimpse of the action. A Confederate army of about the same size was taking up positions along Bull Run Creek near the village of Manassas.

Sherman's fear of his volunteers' lack of training was realized even before the Battle of Bull Run began. (In the South, battles were usually named after the nearest town, so in the Confederacy this first clash was called the Battle of Manassas.) On the march, the men thought nothing of dropping out of line for a drink of water or a little rest in

In July 1861, Bull Run Creek was the site of the first major battle of the Civil War.

the shade. Many ate their rations as they marched, and more had to be ordered forward.

On July 21, 1861, the two amateur armies clashed at Bull Run. At first, the Federals, including Colonel Sherman, who had never before been in a battle, performed surprisingly well. As ordered, he led his brigade toward the center of the Rebel line, pinning down part of the southern army, while other Union troops worked their way around the Rebel flank. Sherman then led a real attack on the center and the Confederate troops reeled backward. Then the Confederate lines suddenly stiffened, inspired by the firm stand of General Thomas Jackson's regiment, a stand that earned Jackson the nickname "Stonewall."

Now the Federals were in retreat. At first it was orderly, but the troops collided with the picnickers, who were trying to get onto the same road. Then an overturned wagon on a bridge caused a jam that panicked the troops. The men now fled with no sense of order, ignoring the shouts of their officers. Sherman remained cool, even as the stampede he had predicted turned the battle into a humiliating defeat. "No curse could be greater than invasion

Thomas "Stonewall" Jackson earned his famous nickname at the Battle of Bull Run.

Sherman was promoted to brigadier general not long after the Battle of Bull Run.

★

In August 1861, Congress promoted Ulysses S. Grant to brigadier general from colonel of volunteers.

★

by a volunteer army," he wrote later. "No [barbarians] ever had less respect for the lives and property of friends and foes."

Back in Washington, Sherman took charge of pulling troops together in case the Confederates followed up their victory by attacking the capital. The next day he went in search of the latest manuals on battlefield tactics to retrain himself so that he could train his men.

The Battle of Bull Run was a day of awakening for the entire nation, more so perhaps for Northerners, who were shocked to discover that this conflict was not going to be a short, glorious, almost bloodless affair. People now had to anticipate a long, costly war with far more dead and wounded than anyone could have imagined. This realization came more slowly to people of the Confederacy; the easy victory at Manassas allowed many to feel they would soon win their independence from the Union.

On the Edge of Madness

In August 1861, the War Department promoted Sherman to brigadier general and ordered him to report to Kentucky. This launched the soldier into a period of strange behavior. Fear of failure or some sense of inadequacy gripped him. Some concluded that he was mentally unbalanced.

The first hint of trouble came soon after his promotion, when he wrote to President Lincoln

The Opening Shots at Fort Sumter

★ ★ ★ ★ ★

The day after Abraham Lincoln was sworn in as president, he received a telegram from Major Robert Anderson, commander of Fort Sumter, requesting more men and supplies. Lincoln did not know what to do. Sumter was a federal fort, but it was located in the harbor of Charleston, South Carolina. Lincoln's cabinet officers warned him that supplying the fort would be regarded by the Confederates as an act of war, and

Robert
Anderson

would allow them to claim that the Union started the war. But Lincoln was afraid that letting the fort go could be considered a recognition of the South's independence.

For six agonizing weeks Lincoln hesitated, while the tension mounted. Citizens and politicians alike demanded action. Finally, Lincoln decided to send only food, and he wired the governor of South Carolina that the supply ships were not warships. Confederate President Jefferson Davis, however, viewed the move as an act of war and sent his orders to the Charleston commander, General P. G. T. Beauregard. Beauregard was ordered to demand that the Federals surrender the fort. Anderson refused.

At 4:30 A.M. on April 12, 1861, Beauregard ordered the shore batteries to open fire. The Civil War had begun. Anderson's men returned the fire, while the relief ships waited outside the harbor. Anderson soon ran out of ammunition. He ordered the already-shredded U.S. flag lowered, and he and his men were evacuated to the supply ships. Anderson was hailed as the North's first hero and was promoted to brigadier general.

In October 1861, the U.S. Navy began construction on the armored warship *Monitor*.
★

that he would like "to serve in a subordinate capacity and in no event to be left in a superior command." Lincoln was sympathetic and sent him to Louisville, Kentucky, where he would be second in command to Brigadier General Robert Anderson, the "Hero of Fort Sumter." Their assignment was to strengthen Union forces in Kentucky to keep the state in the Union. Soon after Sherman arrived, however, Anderson became ill and asked to be relieved of command. Sherman found himself in exactly the position he dreaded—top commander of a force of untrained volunteers.

Something seemed to snap in Sherman's mind. He began to develop unreasonable fears that a military disaster was about to engulf him. He began bombarding the War Department with frantic messages: he needed more troops; Confederate General Albert Sidney Johnston was massing troops to seize Louisville, then invade Ohio and Indiana. (Actually Johnston's force was badly outnumbered and he was worried that Sherman would attack him.)

"To advance would be madness," Sherman wrote, "and to stand still folly.... The idea of going down in History with a Fame such as threatens me nearly makes me crazy, indeed I may be so now." At the hotel where he had his headquarters, passersby could see him endlessly pacing the floor, smoking one cigar after another, his eyes darting about, and his mouth working as he muttered to himself. Rumors spread that he was so exhausted from work and worry that he was losing his mind.

When Secretary of War Simon Cameron arrived in October 1861, Sherman told him he needed 60,000 more men to hold Kentucky and 200,000 to go on the offensive. The numbers Sherman wanted were impossible, and when Cameron told a reporter that he thought Sherman was "unbalanced," the reporter made it worse in his story by referring to Sherman's "insane requests" for 200,000 men.

In early November, Sherman asked to be replaced. An old friend, Brigadier General Don Carlos Buell, was sent to take charge, but Sherman was still despondent. He wrote to John: "If anybody can do better than I can for God's sake let him. I prefer to follow, not to lead, as I confess I have not the confidence of a leader in this war, and would be happy to slide into

ABOVE: Secretary of War Simon Cameron fueled rumors of Sherman's instability by calling Sherman "unbalanced."

BELOW: Don Carlos Buell took over Sherman's command in November 1861.

35

Henry Halleck was a
close friend of Sherman's.

obscurity." And to Ellen, he wrote, "I am almost crazy."

Both Ellen and Senator Sherman were alarmed by the officer's words, and they hurried to Louisville. Their visit seemed to help briefly, but when Buell ordered Sherman to St. Louis, Sherman gloomily predicted as he left that "some terrible disaster is inevitable."

In St. Louis, General Henry Halleck, a friend from California days, tried to ignore the warning signs that the general was having trouble. He sent Sherman on an inspection tour of Union forces in central Missouri. Once again, the fears gripped Sherman and he sent back frantic wires about a huge Confederate army about to attack. A newspaper reported that Sherman was "going about ... with a half-wild expression" and saying that "the Rebels can never be whipped."

Halleck immediately wrote to General George B. McClellan,

George B. McClellan served as commander of all Union armies until Lincoln replaced him in March 1862.

37

A Union navy fleet captured two Confederate forts on Port Royal Sound, South Carolina, in November 1861.

★

who was then commander of all Union armies: "I am satisfied that General Sherman's physical and mental system is so completely broken by labor and care as to render him for the present entirely unfit for duty." Ellen came to take him home to Ohio on a 20-day medical leave.

Although the army had tried to handle the matter quietly, most of the country's newspapers picked up a story in the *Cincinnati Commercial* under the headline, "General William T. Sherman Insane!" Sherman, through his brother-in-law Phil Ewing, wrote a rebuttal, but he felt completely crushed. Once again, he felt he had failed and had brought shame on the Ewing and Sherman families. When his leave was up, he went back to St. Louis, where Halleck put him to work drilling recruits. He wrote to John:

> *I am so sensible now of my disgrace from having exaggerated the force of our enemy in Kentucky that I do think I should have committed suicide were it not for my children. I do not think I can again be entrusted with a command.*

A Powerful Personality

So ended William T. Sherman's first effort at command. He considered himself a failure and much of the public seemed to agree. Some newspaper editors thought he was a coward. Others wrote simply that he was "insane"—a popular 1860s catchall term for all sorts of disorders that were not truly understood.

No matter what the cause of his emotional problems, certain traits were undeniable. He had an intellectual brilliance greater than most other outstanding figures of the Civil War. While intelligence tests were not available in the 1800s, it is quite likely Sherman was in the "genius" range. Another notable aspect of Sherman was the power of his personality. Men—and women— were drawn to him. Despite his psychological problems in 1861, all the military leaders who knew him maintained their confidence in him. Braxton Bragg, P. G. T. Beauregard, Don Carlos Buell, and Henry Halleck—all of whom played major roles in the war—knew that Sherman was an exceptional man who would inspire his troops. They seemed convinced that any difficulties he faced in 1861 were only temporary.

Chapter 3

THE GRANT-SHERMAN PARTNERSHIP

After Bull Run, Union leaders followed a three-pronged attack on the Confederacy. First, the Federal navy established a blockade of the coastline, which prevented the South from shipping its cotton to England and France in exchange for weapons and food supplies. Second, the Union's major army, the Army of the Potomac, intended to march on Richmond, capital of the Confederacy. And third, in the West, the western armies, with the assistance of the navy's gunboats, planned to seize control of the major waterways, including the Mississippi River.

OPPOSITE: Union general Ulysses S. Grant achieved victories over the Confederates in the West.

The Army of the Potomac launched a long, complex campaign against the Rebels who were defending Richmond, but their drives were stopped repeatedly by the Confederate Army of Northern Virginia, commanded by General Robert E. Lee, the South's greatest general.

The one area of progress for Lincoln's government was in the West. In February 1862, Major General Halleck sent Brigadier General Grant to attack Forts Henry and Donelson, which guarded the Tennessee and Cumberland Rivers. Grant's success in capturing both forts broke open the Confederate defensive line and provided the North with its first victories of the war. The victories also

Rebel forces defended the Confederate capital of Richmond, Virginia.

forced the Rebels to withdraw from Kentucky and middle Tennessee.

As Grant was launching his attacks on the forts, Halleck sent Sherman to Paducah, Kentucky, with the task of providing Grant with men, supplies, and ammunition. He performed the task well, and offered to serve under Grant in his next campaign, even though at the moment Sherman was the higher-ranking officer.

After the forts were taken, Halleck formed a new division, put Sherman in command, and assigned him to Grant. It was the start of a Grant-Sherman partnership that soon became a dominant force in the war.

Surprise at Shiloh

With his new division, Sherman was ordered to join Grant at Pittsburg Landing. Sherman's men had heard all the reports about their new commander's nervous breakdown, so they were a little uneasy, but they boarded the steamboats that took them up the Tennessee River to meet Grant.

Halleck gave strict orders not to move farther south against the Confederate army led by General Albert Sidney Johnston until another Federal force under General Buell arrived. That was fine with Grant. Even with Sherman's division, Grant had only about 33,000 men, while Johnston was reported to have 40,000 in his army. It only made sense to wait for Buell's additional 30,000 men before attacking.

43

What neither Grant or Sherman anticipated was that Johnston planned to attack the Union first—before Buell's forces arrived. In fact, the two Union generals had been so confident that they decided to drill some of the raw troops while they waited. They set up camps around a meeting-house called Shiloh Church.

Johnston's men advanced slowly. On the night of April 5, 1862, they were less than a mile from the Union camps. Johnston's officers were so sure the Federals must have heard them that they urged him to call off the attack. But Johnston was determined to strike at dawn.

Some of Sherman's men, including the commander of an Ohio regiment, reported seeing or hearing

The Battle of Shiloh began near this meetinghouse.

Confederates nearby. Sherman refused to believe it. "Take your damned regiment back to Ohio," he joked. "There is no enemy nearer than Corinth."

The Rebels struck at dawn, charging into the camps while some of the soldiers were eating breakfast. The divisions of General Benjamin Prentiss and Sherman were hit hard. One of Prentiss' men recalled that "from right to left, everywhere, it was one never-ending terrible roar, with no prospect of stopping." Some of Sherman's men panicked and ran, but most stayed in position, held by his calm and uncharacteristic optimism.

Throughout the day, Sherman and his men were forced to retreat until they were backed up to the river. The Rebels launched attack after attack but could not break through. They suffered a severe loss when Albert Sidney Johnston was killed. Johnston was only shot in the leg, but there were no doctors nearby and none of the men knew how to tie a tourniquet, so he rapidly bled to death.

During the night, Buell's men arrived on the far side of the river and about 20,000 were ferried across by morning. Grant immediately ordered a counterattack, and within hours,

Albert Sidney Johnston was killed at the Battle of Shiloh.

The Battle of Shiloh resulted in thousands of casualties on both sides.

William T. Sherman

47

the Confederates, now commanded by P. G. T. Beauregard, were in full retreat.

The losses on both sides at the Battle of Shiloh were the highest of the war so far, which shocked people in both the North and South. The Confederates had suffered 10,694 casualties—killed, wounded, and missing; the Federal casualties were 13,047.

P.G.T. Beauregard led the Confederate retreat from Shiloh.

Some newspaper reporters tried to blame Sherman for the heavy losses, invoking his nervous breakdown. But it was hard to find any fault with Sherman. He had rallied his men well, despite having three horses shot from under him and suffering a painful shoulder injury when he toppled from the third horse. Halleck and Grant both praised him for bravery and leadership. In his report, Grant wrote that Sherman "displayed great judgment and skill in the management of his men." Halleck went further: "It was the unanimous opinion here that Brigadier General W. T. Sherman saved the day of [April] 6th and contributed largely to the glorious victory of the 7th."

Sherman did not think he had done anything special, but he was pleased when he was promoted to major general on Halleck's recommendation. That, and the praise in several newspapers, helped to restore his reputation and his confidence. He was able to joke with Ellen: "I have worked hard to keep down, but somehow I am forced into prominence and might as well submit." And to his foster father he wrote proudly, "I know I can take whatever position I choose among my peers."

The newspapers also attacked Grant for the surprise and the heavy losses. He had a reputation as a drinker and some wondered in print if he had been drunk when the Shiloh attack happened. General Halleck reprimanded him and removed him from command. Now it was Grant who was humiliated and ready to quit. Sherman wrote a public letter of support for his friend and persuaded him not to resign. Lincoln, too, stood by Grant, saying, "I can't spare this man. He fights."

Grant, with assistance from Sherman, soon redeemed himself and achieved perhaps his greatest triumph at his next major engagement, the Battle of Vicksburg.

Grant and Sherman at Vicksburg

In October 1862, Grant was again in command of an army, this time with orders to capture Vicksburg, the South's last remaining stronghold on the Mississippi River. Grant immediately asked

Vicksburg, Mississippi, was the South's last remaining stronhold on the Mississippi River.

William T. Sherman

William T. Sherman

Sherman, who was in charge of Memphis, to join him. Together they began working on a plan to seize the city.

The geography of Vicksburg made it perfect for defense. It was perched on a steep bluff above the river, with more than 50 cannons facing the water. This made an attack from the Mississippi impossible. On the landward side, the terrain north and south of the city was marked by deep, narrow ravines; swamps; and impenetrable thickets. The only open route to the city was from the east. This approach was protected by a series of gun emplacements, earthworks, and trenches that Southern engineers had been working on for nearly a year. And defending the fortress city was an army of 30,000 Rebels commanded by General John C. Pemberton.

Tough as Vicksburg was, capturing it was vital to the Union plans. The North already controlled the river north of the city. To the south, Union gunboats and troops had captured New Orleans and held the river as far north as Port Hudson. The remaining 250 miles of the Mississippi, anchored at Vicksburg, prevented the North from controlling the entire river. If Grant could take Vicksburg, it would cut the Confederacy in two and isolate the western states of Louisiana, Arkansas, and Texas.

Late in 1862, Grant and Sherman launched their attack. Grant moved overland into Mississippi to take on about 24,000 of Pemberton's army at Grenada, Mississippi, while Sherman moved south from Memphis with 30,000 men loaded on steamboats.

John C. Pemberton led Rebel forces who defended Vicksburg.

The attack was a complete failure. Sherman landed his men north of Vicksburg, where he faced a strong Confederate outpost at Chickasaw Bayou. He waited for word from Grant, not knowing that Rebel cavalry had destroyed Grant's supply base and forced him to withdraw to Tennessee.

Sherman didn't know what to do. He feared that delay would be ruinous, so he tried to launch his own part of the attack late in December. The Rebels were in a strong position, with the Union troops forced to struggle through dense thickets. He quickly called off the attack after losing nearly 1,800 men to only 187 Confederates.

During the remaining winter months, Grant tried to have his men dig canals that would use the Mississippi's water to get them east of Vicksburg. The digging might have been good exercise, but it did not produce a workable canal.

In April 1863, Grant carried out several brilliant maneuvers that got him east of the city. Sherman, by

53

bluffing another attack from the north, kept the defenders guessing. In just 17 days, Grant had marched his men 180 miles through enemy territory, fought five battles against separate forces, and inflicted 7,200 casualties, double his own losses.

These bold moves by Grant greatly impressed Sherman. Speaking to a friend about Grant's maneuvers to get at Vicksburg, Sherman said:

> I am a much brighter man than Grant; I can see things quicker than he can, and I know more about books than he does, but I'll tell you where he beats me, and where he beats the world: he don't care a cent for what he can't see the enemy doing, but it scares me like Hell.

While Grant moved west toward Vicksburg, he sent Sherman to the city of Jackson, the state capital, 40 miles from Vicksburg. In Jackson, another Confederate general named Johnston (Joseph E.) had a small force. Johnston retreated, abandoning the city, and Sherman had his men destroy the railroad tracks and terminal, as well as all public buildings. He then joined Grant at Vicksburg, which brought their combined force to nearly 70,000 men.

After two frontal attacks on the Vicksburg defenses failed late in May, Grant settled in for a siege of the city. For the next six weeks, Pemberton's 30,000 men and about 4,000 civilians were trapped, living with daily bombardment from

The Battle of Vicksburg finally ended when Rebel forces surrendered on July 3, 1863.

Federal cannons, and coming closer to starvation each day.

Finally, on July 3, 1863, Pemberton agreed to surrender his army and the city. The formal signing was the next day—July 4th, Independence Day.

At the same time, another drama was unfolding in Gettysburg, Pennsylvania. In a bold move, General Robert E. Lee tried to change the momentum of the war by invading a state in the North. In a three-day battle, perhaps the most dramatic of the war, Union troops drove back

55

every Rebel attack. With one-third of his proud Army of Northern Virginia dead, wounded, or missing, Lee headed back to Virginia on the very day Pemberton surrendered at Vicksburg.

The two Federal victories—Vicksburg and Gettysburg—marked the most significant turning point in the war. The Confederates were now on the defensive. Their best hope of winning their independence was to keep the war going until war-weariness overwhelmed the North. This meant keeping Lee's army in action in the East, another army in the West, and holding onto two key cities—Richmond in the East and Atlanta in the West.

Robert E. Lee

Sherman's New Concept of War

After the heady triumph at Vicksburg, Grant sent Sherman—commanding seven divisions—to take care of General Joseph E. Johnston's small force at Jackson. After a brief battle, Johnston withdrew and Sherman turned his men loose to destroy the town. They did a thorough job. In his report to Grant, he wrote: "Jackson will no longer be a

The Battle of Gettysburg was a turning point in the war.

point of danger. The inhabitants are subjugated. They cry aloud for mercy. The land is devastated for 30 miles around."

Sherman was beginning to see how effective destructive raids could be. By destroying railroads, supplies, and warehouses, he was attacking the Rebels' ability to fight. And, when his men laid waste to the countryside, they drained the Southerners' will to fight.

Although Sherman did not know it, he was waging war the way it would be waged through the 20th century. This was "total war" against an enemy's entire population and its economy. Sherman was well aware that this was a particularly cruel kind of war, yet he saw no other strategy for success. "If the Southerners cannot be made to love us," he wrote, "they can be made to fear us [by making] war so terrible that they will realize the fact that, however brave and gallant and devoted to their country, still they are mortal."

At the same time, Sherman tried to make sure that his men didn't inflict needless pain and that they did not harm civilians or their personal property. In orders to his troops, he said:

> *This demoralising and disgraceful practice of pillage [looting] must cease, else the country will rise on us and justly shoot us down like dogs and wild beasts.*

Sherman's men destroy a railroad near Atlanta.

Toward the Final Campaign

Although the South had been devastated by the defeats at Vicksburg and Gettysburg, the people of the Confederacy were far from surrender. They still had about 200,000 men in uniform. They also had the advantage of fighting on the defensive—the North had to come to them, extending their supply lines farther and farther, and fighting in unfamiliar territory.

The Battle of Chickamauga in southern Tennessee in September 1863 was an example of the Confederates' ability to sustain the war. Confederate General Braxton Bragg led a Rebel army against a Union force commanded by General William Rosecrans and won a huge victory, some said the biggest Confederate victory of the war. The Federals retreated in panic and the entire army might have been lost except for a heroic stand by General George Thomas and his men—a feat that earned Thomas the nickname the "Rock of Chickamauga."

ABOVE: Braxton Bragg
BELOW: William Rosecrans

59

Rosecrans managed to retreat into Chattanooga, where Bragg took advantage of the rugged hills, mountains, and rivers to trap him there. Over the next month, the battered Union army was under siege, unable to move out or get supplies in. In October, Lincoln and the War Department put Grant in charge of all Union forces in the West and sent him first to Chattanooga to try to save the Union forces trapped there. Grant

George Thomas

William T. Sherman

The Battle of Chickamauga was a decisive victory for the Confederacy.

used the opportunity to demonstrate his genius again. He relieved Rosecrans of command and named Thomas to replace him. He sent a telegram to Sherman ordering him to come to Chattanooga with the 20,000 men in his command at Nashville.

When Grant arrived in Chattanooga late in October, he found the troops suffering from scurvy and starvation, with dead mules and horses scattered everywhere. He devised a route to get supplies in and planned an attack to overcome Bragg's Rebels, who controlled the hills overlooking the city, including the strategically important Missionary Ridge.

61

Grant's main assault on Missionary Ridge was preceded by the Battle of Lookout Mountain (pictured).

As Sherman and his men arrived, Grant intended for him to lead the main assault on Missionary Ridge, where the largest part of Bragg's army was located. Sherman's men had to make a dangerous nighttime crossing of the Tennessee River on

pontoon boats. In describing that crossing on the night of November 23, 1863, one of Sherman's men revealed how highly they regarded their general:

We had marched 20 miles a day to reach Chattanooga. Now this corps was to form the left of Grant's forces, cross a deep river in the darkness and assault the nearly inaccessible position of Bragg's army.... At two o'clock we heard some splashing in the water... the [116 pontoon] boats had come for us.... Quietly, two by two, we slipped down to the water's edge and stepped into the rude flatboats.

"There's room for thirty in a boat," said a tall man... who stood on the bank near us in the darkness.

William T. Sherman

Joseph Hooker was a Union commander at the Battle of Chattanooga.

Few of us had ever before heard the voice of our beloved commander. Sherman's personal presence, his sharing the danger we were about to undertake gave us confidence.

The assault on Missionary Ridge did not go the way Sherman or Grant had planned. Sherman's men attacked in the morning but, by midday, they found they had only captured an outlying hill. They were separated from the main ridge by a narrow ravine that did not show on the maps.

Grant saw that the attack on his right flank, led by General Joe Hooker, had also bogged down. To relieve the pressure on Sherman and Hooker, Grant ordered his largest force, under Thomas, to charge partway up the center of Missionary Ridge. In one of the most dramatic episodes of the war, Thomas's troops stormed up the hill and, instead of stopping partway, as they had been ordered, they scrambled wildly on up the steep slope. The Rebel defenders were overwhelmed and retreated in panic. When the Federals reached the crest of the ridge, the Confederates were fleeing for their lives down the other side.

Chapter 4

"THE WAR NOW BEGINS"

After Chattanooga, Lincoln and his administration could not do enough to show their appreciation for Grant's accomplishments. Congress had a gold medal struck in his honor and restored the rank of Lieutenant General, which had been held in the past only by George Washington and Winfield Scott (hero of the Mexican War). More important, Lincoln placed Grant in charge of all Union forces.

OPPOSITE: In 1864, Sherman received orders to capture Atlanta and force the Confederate Army of Tennessee to surrender.

William T. Sherman

> ★
> In January 1864, Arkansas adopted an antislavery constitution.
> ★

Early in 1864, Grant went to Washington to receive his honors and to discuss with the president his plans for ending the war. Grant would remain in the East, making his headquarters with the Army of the Potomac. The objective in the East would be to capture Richmond, the capital of the Confederacy, and force the surrender of Robert E. Lee and his Army of Northern Virginia.

In the West, Grant placed Sherman in command of the three armies that had been operating there. His goal would be to capture Atlanta and force the surrender of the Confederate Army of Tennessee. Sherman, who had resisted being in command, relished his new position and was eager to start, as if he felt that everything in his life had been guiding him to this moment. In a letter to Ellen, he wrote, "All that has gone before is mere skirmishing. The war now begins."

The Battle Plan

In March 1864, Sherman and Grant met in Cincinnati's Burnet House Hotel, filling the room with cigar smoke that forced aides to excuse themselves to get air now and then. The generals knew that the final campaign of the war was in their hands, and both felt confident of victory.

The two men agreed that, after a month of preparation, they would both start their advance at the same time and neither would pause until they had won.

William T. Sherman

Grant's orders to Sherman helped to shape his strategy. Grant told him "to move against the Confederate army, to break it up, and to get into the interior of the enemy's country as far as you can, inflicting all the damage you can against their war resources." For Sherman, these orders meant Atlanta as well as the Rebel army. "Atlanta," he wrote, "was too important a place in the hands of the enemy to be left undisturbed, with its magazines,

Joseph Johnston

stores, workshops, foundries and more especially its railroads."

The personalities of the generals made warfare in the West very different from that in the East. In the East, Lee and Grant were both fighters who sought to crush the enemy. In the West, where General Joseph Johnston had replaced Bragg, both Johnston and Sherman preferred a war of maneuver, fighting head-on only when necessary to gain a

better position—or to prevent the enemy
from gaining one. These differences usually
led to heavier casualties in the East. In the
4 months leading to September 2, 1864,
the day Sherman took Atlanta, each side in
the West suffered about 30,000 casualties;
in Virginia, Lee's forces, fighting much of
the time from trenches, had about 40,000
casualties, while Grant's army, usually on
the attack, had losses of almost 75,000.

Sherman and Johnston Prepare for the Showdown

When General Joe Johnston took command of the
South's Army of Tennessee, he knew that President
Jefferson Davis disliked him and, in some ways,
hoped that he would fail. He also knew that
Sherman's armies, about to descend on him,
outnumbered his men by almost two to one. In
addition, Chattanooga was now a Federal stronghold, protected by the rugged Cumberland
Mountains and the Tennessee River. Despite
these obstacles, Davis expected him to attack the
Federals; "prompt and vigorous action" was needed
for "re-occupying Tennessee," he said.

Johnston proceeded with his command, doing
things his way. The men he commanded had
suffered the humiliation of the drubbing at
Missionary Ridge so he did whatever he could
to build up morale, demanding fresh uniforms,
shoes for those who needed them, and better

William T. Sherman

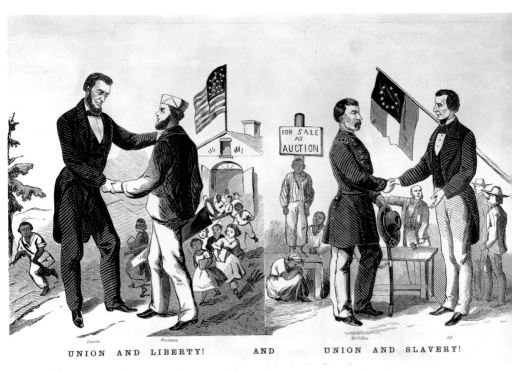

UNION AND LIBERTY!   AND   UNION AND SLAVERY!

This poster is from Abraham Lincoln's re-election campaign in 1864.

rations. Discipline was also improved and, by spring, the Army of Tennessee was ready to take on the Yankees.

One element in the South's favor was time, as war weariness was beginning to affect the North. If the Rebels could prevent a major Union victory before the presidential election in November 1864, the "Copperheads" (Southern sympathizers) in the North might persuade voters that the South could not be beaten; the popular General George McClellan as the "peace candidate" could beat Lincoln's bid for re-election. Johnston was confident he could prevent Sherman from taking Atlanta before November.

71

For his part, Sherman, in Chattanooga preparing for his invasion of Georgia, was equally confident that he would be in Atlanta well before the election. Now that he was sure of himself as a commander, and had battle-hardened troops to work with, he quickly proved that he was a brilliant strategist.

First, he made two moves that other generals did not consider. One move was to strengthen the defense of the single railroad line that connected Chattanooga with Nashville and Louisville. This was his major supply line and he could not afford to have it cut by a Rebel cavalry raid, so he had outposts established along the line to warn of any approaching attack.

His second move was to have rails, ties, and equipment brought close to his advancing army. As he advanced into northern Georgia, he was sure the Confederates would destroy the railroad to Atlanta as they retreated; Sherman's men would be able to rebuild the railroad as they advanced. Because of this planning, his army was never short of food, ammunition, or other supplies. Historians have called this "the greatest logistical achievement of the war."

Sherman had three armies to work with, and he kept them intact. The largest of the three forces was the Army of the Tennessee—which he had commanded at Missionary Ridge. He placed Major General James B. McPherson, one of the most

William T. Sherman

popular and talented Union commanders, in charge. The tough, experienced Army of the Cumberland was nearly as large. Sherman entrusted it to General Thomas. The Army of the Ohio, with little more than 20,000 men, was commanded by General John M. Schofield. Combined, the three armies totaled more than 100,000, while Johnston had roughly 60,000.

The Battle for Atlanta

On May 5, 1864, while Grant began his move against Lee in Virginia, Sherman led his army out of Chattanooga toward Atlanta, 100 miles away. Johnston's men were dug in on a long, rugged hill called Rocky Face Ridge.

Sherman advanced directly toward Johnston's force with two-thirds of his army. He had no intention of fighting a pitched battle; instead, he sent the other third of his army circling to the South around the Confederate flank, hoping to get between Johnston and Atlanta.

Johnston saw what was happening and ordered a retreat to the town of Resaca, and this established a pattern for the conflict. Through May and June, Sherman and Johnston transformed the mountains and valleys of northern Georgia into a giant chessboard. Sherman would advance on the Rebels' entrenched position and send one corps around the Confederates' flank. Except for sharp skirmishes, there was no full-scale battle. To avoid

73

William T. Sherman

being trapped, Johnston would again slide back to other prepared positions closer to Atlanta.

Sherman's ability to maneuver, with 100,000 men divided into three armies, impressed his own men. These veteran troops had seen enough bloody fighting that they could appreciate advancing 10 or 12 miles by marching, without shooting. Their affection for their commander grew and they were soon referring to him as "Uncle Billy" or by his boyhood nickname, "Cump."

By mid-June, the Confederates had retreated to a position anchored by Kennesaw Mountain, only 20 miles from Atlanta. The steep, forested mountain rose abruptly from a plain, dominating the surrounding countryside. The mountain's two peaks, Sherman wrote, were "crowned with

Federal forces attacked Confederate defenses at the Battle of Kennesaw Mountain.

batteries, and the spurs [leading to the peaks] were alive with men busy felling trees, digging pits, and preparing for the grand struggle impending."

Sherman made one of his worst blunders of the war when he chose to ignore Johnston's strong defensive position and ordered an attack on June 27, 1864. In his memoirs, Sherman described the short, disastrous Battle of Kennesaw Mountain:

In June 1864, Congress passed the Internal Revenue Act in order to increase funding for the war.

> About 9 o'clock A.M. . . . the troops moved to the assault and all along our lines for ten miles a furious fire of artillery and musketry was kept up. At all points the enemy met us with determined courage and in great force. By 11:30 the assault was over, and had failed.

A Confederate soldier provided the Rebels' view of the three futile Union assaults:

> A solid line of blue came up the hill. My pen is unable to describe the scene of carnage that ensued in the next two hours. Column after column of Federal soldiers were crowded upon that line. No sooner would a regiment mount our works than they were shot down or surrendered. Yet still they came . . . . I am satisfied that every man in our regiment killed . . . fivescore men. All that was necessary was to load and shoot. In fact, I will ever think that the reason they did not capture our works was the impossibility of their living men to pass over the bodies of their dead.

75

Another Confederate recalled the aftermath of the two-hour battle:

When the Yankees fell back and the firing ceased, I never saw so many broken down and exhausted men in my life. I was sick as a horse, and as wet with blood and sweat as I could be, and many of our men were vomiting with excessive fatigue; our tongues were parched and cracked for water, and our faces blackened with powder and smoke . . . .

The Union losses were 2,000 killed or wounded and 52 missing—one out of every eight men who took part in the attack. The Confederate losses were 270 killed or wounded and 172 missing. Despite the horrific losses, Sherman remained focused on his goal. His wife, Ellen, remained his confidant even in the midst of military campaigns. As he became accustomed to the horrors of the war, he said things to her that he would not have revealed to anyone else. After the Kennesaw Mountain disaster, he wrote to her: "I begin to regard the death and mangling of a couple of thousand men as a small affair, a kind of morning dash."

Sherman had learned that it was useless to continue frontal assaults and he returned to his tactic of flanking. Johnston, in turn, retreated still closer to Atlanta. Early in July, the Southerners crossed the Chattahoochee River, just 5 miles from Atlanta, and, on July 10, entered their trenches and earthworks surrounding Atlanta.

Johnston and his men were confident they could hold Atlanta indefinitely.

Jefferson Davis, however, had given up on Johnston, primarily because he refused to attack. Although Johnston noted that his retreating tactics were precisely the same as those for which Lee was being praised in the East, Davis dismissed him on July 17. The Confederate soldiers were in tears when they learned that he was leaving. "This act," one of the men recalled, "threw a damper over this army from which it never recovered."

Johnston's replacement was General John Bell Hood. He had never commanded a full army but he was Davis's favorite kind of general—a fighter. Hood had lost the use of an arm from a wound received at Gettysburg, and then lost a leg at Chickamauga. He had to be strapped to his saddle, but he had lost none of his combative spirit.

Sherman was delighted with Hood's appointment because he knew it would mean reckless attacks against the Federal line. And Hood didn't waste any time. On July 20, he attacked Thomas's army. After being turned back on that flank,

John Bell Hood replaced Joseph Johnston as commander of the Army of Tennessee.

he lunged at McPherson's force on July 21. Sherman and McPherson together directed the defense against Hood's assault, until McPherson went to see if a gap in the lines had been closed. On his way back to Sherman, he encountered Rebel soldiers who motioned him to surrender. Instead, McPherson politely tipped his hat and spurred his horse. The Confederates opened fire, and a single bullet killed him instantly. The Union soldiers were amazed to see Sherman weep openly when McPherson's body was brought in.

By late July, Sherman had Atlanta under siege. In the first ten days under Hood, the Confederates had suffered 18,000 killed, wounded, or missing—roughly one-third of Hood's Army of Tennessee.

On September 2, Hood was forced to give up Atlanta, and Sherman's troops moved in. It was a devastating loss for the South. The city anchored the western and southern parts of the Confederacy, with vital rail connections reaching in all directions; its factories, producing weapons and equipment, were lost. And, unable to remove the huge stores of munitions, Hood had them blown up in a mighty explosion that could be heard for miles.

"So Atlanta is ours and fairly won," Sherman telegraphed to Lincoln on September 2, 1864. Lincoln wrote a letter of congratulations, saying

Sherman (leaning on back of cannon) and his men survey weapons left behind in Atlanta.

that Sherman's maneuvering and battles would make the campaign "famous in the annals of war... [and] entitled all those who have partici-pated therein to the applause and thanks of the nation." He designated September 5 a "national day of celebration" and commissioned Sherman a major general in the regular army.

Grant, in his official report, added his praise:

> General Sherman's movement from Chattanooga was prompt, skillful, and brilliant. The history of his flank movements and battles... will ever be read with an interest unsurpassed by anything [similar] in history.

The taking of Atlanta also made Lincoln's re-election all but a sure thing. For months, the

79

president himself had been quite certain he would lose, and Grant being stalled by Lee had added to the doubts. Sherman's triumph changed everything.

Sherman's next move was to have the entire civilian population evacuated from Atlanta. Hood and the city's civilian leaders protested. Sherman's reply stated again his approach to war: "War is cruelty and you cannot refine it.... You might as well appeal against the thunder-storm as against these terrible hardships." Beginning on September 12, he allowed a ten-day truce to remove the nearly 2,000 adults and children.

Sherman expected that Hood would still try to keep the Federals from pushing deeper into Georgia. Instead, Davis ordered him to move into Tennessee, where he could attack the Union's long supply line. Davis was confident that this strategy would succeed. Late in September, he declared that "Sherman cannot keep up his long line of communication, and retreat sooner or later he must."

The March to the Sea

Sherman, however, decided not to go after Hood. Instead, he proposed marching through Georgia to the Atlantic coast, destroying as much of the state's war resources as possible. Grant and Lincoln were apprehensive, but felt they had to rely on Sherman's judgment.

While Sherman prepared to depart Atlanta with 62,000 men, he sent generals Thomas and Schofield

Sherman departed Atlanta with 62,000 men to begin his "March to the Sea."

with the rest of the army to take care of Hood.
First, at the Battle of Franklin in Tennessee, Hood
attacked Schofield's army even though his infantry
was forced to cross two miles of open fields. It
was a courageous but useless charge and, in a few
hours time, Hood lost 6,252 men—killed,
wounded, or missing—including six generals.

Schofield then joined Thomas at Nashville.
Together they had nearly 60,000 men. Hood, with
barely half that number, had run out of options.
Grant, however, was worried that Hood might
break loose, race north or east, and cause serious
trouble. He did not realize that Hood's army was
close to breaking apart and he never did understand
that Thomas was one of the best generals in the
army. Grant was about to have Thomas dismissed
when the "Rock of Chickamauga" made his move.

81

That "Devil Forrest"

While Sherman's army was slowly advancing toward Atlanta, their commander's greatest worry was his long supply line. And the man he most feared as a menace to that line was the South's great cavalry officer, General Nathan Bedford Forrest. Forrest entered the army as a private but rose rapidly to the rank of major general. He used his cavalry as mounted foot soldiers; instead of old-fashioned cavalry charges, the men rode swiftly into position to surprise the enemy, then attacked as infantry.

On June 10, 1864, Forrest's 3,300 men met a Union force of 8,000 sent by Sherman at Brice's Crossroads. In the daylong fight, the Federals were badly beaten. "Forrest is the very devil," Sherman wrote, and said he should be hounded "to the death, if it cost 10,000 lives and break the Treasury. There never will be peace in Tennessee till Forrest is dead." Forrest and his cavalry tried to help General Hood at the Battle of Franklin and again at Nashville, but he never repeated the success of Brice's Crossroads.

On December 15 and 16 Thomas and Schofield all but destroyed what was left of the Army of Tennessee, sending it in headlong flight to the south. Hood's army no longer existed as an effective fighting force.

President Lincoln appointed Salmon P. Chase as chief justice of the Supreme Court in December 1864.

In the meantime, Sherman had started his famous "March to the Sea" in mid-November. His men were to march in two columns on a 60-mile-wide front from Atlanta to the port of Savannah, 255 miles away. The army's wagon train, which stretched for more than 20 miles, included more than 2,000 mule teams, six mules in each team.

As they left Atlanta, Sherman gave the order to torch the city, intending to burn only the factories, storehouses, and other buildings that had any possible military use. His men were free and easy with their firebrands, however, and nearly 2,000 buildings were destroyed. Major George Nichols, one of the last to leave, described the scene:

> ... The heaven is one expanse of lurid fire; the air is filled with flying, burning cinders; buildings covering two hundred acres are in ruins or in flames; every instant there is the sharp detonation or the smothered booming sound of exploding shells and powder concealed in the buildings.... These are machine shops where have been forged and cast the Rebel cannon, shot and shell that have carried death to many a brave defender of our nation's honor....

83

MARCHING THROUGH GEORGIA

Sherman's men cut a 60-mile-wide swath of destruction through Georgia.

The burning of Atlanta horrified Southerners, who saw the act as a symbol of the North's barbarism, a symbol that would smolder in their minds for many years. "My aim," Sherman said later, "was to whip the Rebels...make them fear and dread us." He succeeded in that, but to the people of the South, he became "that ghoul, that hyena," "the Burner," and "the Killer," and his men were called "scabs, scavengers, and the scum of creation."

And that was only the beginning of Sherman's campaign. During the weeks that followed, his men went on a rampage as they cut their 60-mile-wide swath of destruction through Georgia. His foragers, also known as "Bummers" and "smoke-house rangers," brought back cattle, chickens, turkeys, pigs, all sorts of vegetables and grain,

plus sugar, coffee, and liquor. What they couldn't
consume or carry, they destroyed. At night, they
built huge bonfires, ate lavish meals, played cards,
and listened to the bands play hymns, ballads,
and rousing marching songs. In one town, they
broke into a bank and used stacks of Confederate
currency to build fires for brewing their morning
coffee. The Union's picnic-like atmosphere
irritated Southerners even more than if their
enemies had been openly vengeful or angry.

In addition to the Bummers, who made up
only a small portion of Sherman's army, his main
troops went to work destroying anything that
might possible be useful for war, including
crops, barns, public buildings, and all railroad
equipment. Nearly 300 miles of the Georgia
Central Railroad were torn up. The wooden ties

Sherman's army tore up nearly 300 miles of railroad tracks throughout Georgia.

were piled in great heaps and set on fire; the iron rails were placed on the flames until they were hot enough to bend; they were then lifted off the fire with big wrenches, and twisted around trees, creating what the men called "Sherman hairpins" or "Jeff Davis neckties." Once the iron cooled, the rails were impossible to straighten.

For more than a month, no one knew exactly where Sherman and his army were—he had effectively cut off all communication with the outside world. Grant told reporters that Sherman's army was like a mole burrowing under a lawn: "You can here and there trace his track, but you are not quite certain where he will come out until you see his head."

On December 10, 1864, Sherman's army emerged outside Savannah. At Fort McAllister, south of the city, 18,000 Confederate troops stood in his way. But the Federal troops charged under heavy fire across rice fields loaded with mines, and quickly captured the fort. A few days later, Confederate General William Hardee pulled his troops out of Savannah, and Sherman's proud army in sparkling blue uniforms marched in. On December 22, Sherman sent his famous telegram to Lincoln: "I beg

William Hardee evacuated his troops from Savannah as Sherman closed in.

William T. Sherman

to present you, as a Christmas gift, the city of Savannah, with 150 heavy guns and plenty of ammunition, and also about 25,000 bales of cotton."

Perspectives on Sherman's March

Since historic times, armies have been destructive when marching through enemy territory, and that has included living off the land by taking crops and farm animals. Sherman's March to the Sea, however, changed the rules. The concept of total war meant widespread destruction of any potential war resources, but even Sherman expected his men to respect private property—except for food items.

Members of Sherman's army raid a Southern plantation.

"Damn the Torpedoes!"

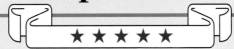

★ ★ ★ ★ ★

In addition to the seizure of Atlanta in the late summer of 1864, the Union won another stirring victory in the Battle of Mobile Bay in August. It was the greatest naval battle of the war. The Rebels had laced the harbor with mines—called torpedoes in the Civil War—but Admiral David Farragut ordered his ships to advance. "Damn the torpedoes!" he shouted. "Full speed ahead!" His flagship was hit by shot after shot, "mowing down the men, deluging the decks with blood, and scattering mangled fragments of humanity so thickly that it was difficult to stand on the deck." Farragut had himself lashed to the rigging so he wouldn't be swept overboard.

By the end of August, Mobile Bay was sealed—no Confederate ships could get in or out, and the Union navy controlled the entire Gulf of Mexico. The defeat was another disaster for the Confederacy. In the North, people were thrilled by news of the victory, its drama, and Farragut's heroic order to "Damn the torpedoes!" Combined with the capture of Atlanta, it helped to greatly reinvigorate Union morale.

The Bummers in Sherman's army, however, tended to ignore his rules about plundering homes and farms. Some even tortured homeowners until they revealed the hiding places of valuables. Sherman recognized that the foraging parties went too far. "No doubt," he wrote, "many acts of pillage, robbery and violence were committed.... But," he added defensively, "these acts were exceptional and incidental."

A young Georgian named Eliza Andrews disagreed with Sherman's characterizations. She wrote in her diary:

★
Actor John Wilkes Booth tried to kidnap President Lincoln on several occasions during 1864, but was unsuccessful each time.
★

> ...About three miles from Sparta, Georgia, we struck the "burnt country".... There was hardly a fence left standing.... The fields were trampled down and the road was lined with carcasses of horses, hogs and cattle that the invaders, unable either to consume or carry away with them, had wantonly shot down, to starve out the people and prevent them from making their crops. The stench in some places was unbearable.... The dwellings that were standing all showed signs of pillage...here and there lone chimney stacks, "Sherman's sentinels"; told of homes lain in ashes. The infamous wretches! I couldn't wonder now that those poor people should want to put a rope around the neck of every red-handed devil of 'em.

Many of the soldiers felt the people of the South had started the war and had brought the destruction

89

Contrabands—escaped slaves—traveled with Sherman's army.

on themselves. Others felt that the Bummers went too far, and some even provided help for people who had been robbed or burned out.

Thousands of former slaves followed after the Federal army, eager to follow what likely seemed to be the road to freedom. The freed slaves—often 25,000 or more at a time—willingly took on camp chores, or helped with the destruction of railroads. They were in awe of Sherman, their liberator, and called him "Angel of the Lord" and "the man that rules the world." And, in Savannah, a reporter wrote: "How gloriously it sounded . . . the 'Freedmen's Battle Hymn' . . . sung by 500 freedmen in the Savannah slave market, where some of the singers had been sold in days gone by."

At the coast, the Union troops enjoyed a change of diet. As one Federal soldier wrote, his earlier diet of "beefsteak, porksteak, broiled chicken, and sweet potatoes," was changed to "oyster soup, oysters on the half shell, roast goose, fried oysters, rice, raisins, coffee, and roast oysters."

★

In February 1865, Union soldiers occupied the last open Confederate port, in Wilmington, North Carolina.

★

The End of the War

On February 1, 1865, Sherman moved north from Savannah, heading toward Grant's army, which was still trying to corner the ragged, half-starved Rebels serving under Robert E. Lee. As Sherman's army entered South Carolina, Davis and other Confederate leaders thought it would take months for them to advance through the swampy lowlands, with the many rivers swollen by winter rains. But, after nearly four years of war, Sherman's tough veterans had learned to fell trees and make roads through the swamps. They traveled through South Carolina as fast as they had through Georgia. On February 17, they took Columbia; by March 21, they were 425 miles from Savannah.

In a desperate effort to keep the Confederacy alive, Lee was placed in supreme command of whatever troops were left. He brought Johnston out of retirement and hoped Johnston, with a ragtag force of about 30,000 men, could somehow stop Sherman. "I can do no more than annoy him," Johnston said.

Sherman's men, once they entered South Carolina, destroyed property even more

91

William T. Sherman

Sherman's men destroyed property in South Carolina even more energetically than they had in Georgia.

ferociously than they had in Georgia. Like most Northerners, they considered South Carolina the heart of the Confederacy, and it was the first state to secede, so it deserved whatever punishment they could deliver.

By the end of March, Federal soldiers were amazed that the Rebels that faced them could still fight. Lee's Army of Northern Virginia, all but surrounded at Petersburg, Virginia, had only about 25,000 men left, and these were scarecrow soldiers, dressed in rags, half-starved—but still fighting. Lee had the nerve to plan a breakout, which would enable him to join forces with Johnston. Together, with more than 50,000 men, he wanted to move deeper into the South and keep the war going.

There was simply too much Union power arrayed against them for Lee's scheme to work. Grant's army now numbered 120,000, and Sherman, joined by Schofield, had nearly 100,000 men. In addition, Sherman's men, moving north rapidly, planned to connect with Grant's force for what they thought would be the final battle.

There was no real final battle; instead, the Confederacy expired in a series of spasms as Lee tried to break away from Grant. For two weeks, Grant's troops advanced trench by trench through the Rebel lines, each day's struggle sometimes ending in frantic hand-to-hand fighting. On April 9, 1865, Lee finally surrendered to Grant at Appomattox Court House.

A few days later, Sherman's army clashed with Johnston's much smaller force in North Carolina and easily forced the patched-together Rebel army to retreat. Sherman did not bother to pursue Johnston, knowing that the end had come. On April 26, 1865, Johnston surrendered to Sherman at Durham Station, North Carolina, officially

Sherman's men triumphantly raised the Union flag over the State House in Columbia, South Carolina.

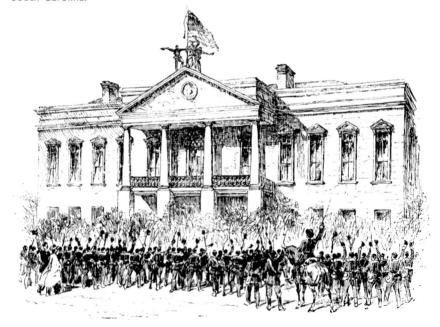

In April 1865, Lee surrendered to Grant in Appomattox Court House, Virginia, ending the Civil War.

William T. Sherman

William T. Sherman

John Wilkes Booth, who assassinated President Lincoln, was killed on the same day Johnston surrendered to Sherman.

ending Rebel resistance, although Lee's surrender to Grant seventeen days earlier had effectively ended the war.

On the day Johnston surrendered, an actor named John Wilkes Booth was surrounded by soldiers and a posse; Booth was killed, either by his own hand or by one of the men in pursuit. On the night of April 14, Booth had added to the great national tragedy when he assassinated President Lincoln, apparently with the notion that he was helping the Confederate cause.

As Americans mourned the loss of their great president, they began to reconstruct the war-ravaged South and search for ways to heal the wounds of a battered nation.

POSTSCRIPT: FINDING SHERMAN'S PLACE IN HISTORY

Sherman's career story after the Civil War is quickly told:

The peace terms he made with General Johnston were remarkably lenient. Like Grant, Sherman hated war, and both generals treated the defeated Confederates with honor and respect. Sherman, however, had included arrangements for restoring the Confederate states to the Union. This was a political decision that was not a matter for the military to decide; consequently, the government rejected Sherman's treaty. Sherman accepted this but he always felt that the government had been heavy-handed in the way he was treated.

He returned to St. Louis and remained in the army, helping in the construction of the Transcontinental Railroad and contributing to establishing peace with Plains Indian tribes. Sherman was promoted to lieutenant general in 1866 and, when his friend Ulysses S. Grant became president in 1869, assumed command of the entire army. He held that position until 1883, then retired from active duty. He died in New York City on February 14, 1891.

After the Civil War, Sherman worked on the Transcontinental Railroad. This picture shows the ceremony at Promontory Point, Utah, which marked the completion of the railroad in 1869.

Sherman's famous statement, "War is hell!" was not made during the war, but during a speech in 1880. He made another famous statement in 1884 when his name was offered at the Republican National Convention as a possible presidential candidate. "If nominated," he declared, "I will not accept. If elected, I will not serve."

William Tecumseh Sherman's rank among the generals of the Civil War is not at all clear. Most historians place Lee and Grant far above all others, with Lee usually given the edge as the greatest leader and strategist. If Sherman is ranked third, most historians make him a distant third.

Sherman's critics point out that he never commanded a full army until 1864, when the Confederacy was already seriously weakened. They also argue that he lost more often than he won. His first attack at Vicksburg, for example, was a disaster; at Missionary Ridge, he became bogged down when Grant expected his corps to lead the attack; and, at Kennesaw Mountain, he ordered an attack that handed Johnston's Rebels a one-sided victory. Finally, doubts remain about Sherman's destructive marches through Georgia and South Carolina. Some historians believe that these did nothing to shorten the war.

There is also much that can be said in Sherman's favor. First, no general on either side showed greater skill in moving and supplying a large army over an area that stretched from Nashville to Chattanooga, then through Atlanta to Savannah. No matter how long his lines of communication and supply became, his men always had ample food, weapons, ammunition, and other supplies.

William T. Sherman, later in life

99

Second, Sherman's approach to Atlanta revealed his skill as a strategist. By constant maneuvering, he forced Johnston's army into steady retreats and, except for the mistake at Kennesaw Mountain, avoided a frontal assault that would have resulted in thousands more killed and wounded.

Then, while Grant remained bogged down before Richmond and Petersburg, Sherman managed to capture Atlanta at a critical time. In the summer of 1864, war weariness was sapping the fighting spirit of the North and Lincoln's re-election was seriously in doubt. "I am going to be beaten," Lincoln told a friend in August, "and unless some great change takes place, badly beaten." On September 2, Sherman's army marched into Atlanta, and Lincoln won re-election in November.

Finally, it can be argued that Sherman's marches through Georgia and South Carolina ushered in the era of modern warfare by making the enemy's entire homeland part of the war. This is the philosophy of war that was used in the following century to justify the bombing of civilian populations and cities in order to reduce the ability and the will to wage war. The evidence, however, suggests that such tactics actually increase the enemy's determination to keep fighting.

The conflicting opinions over Sherman's contributions to the Civil War will likely not be resolved soon, if ever. It is indisputable, however, that Sherman was a pivotal figure in our nation's history.

Glossary

amateur A beginner, not a professional.

annex To add.

brigade A military unit smaller than a division, usually consisting of three to five regiments of 500–1,000 soldiers.

cavalry Soldiers on horseback.

earthworks A raised structure made of earth or dirt—used to make a strong fort.

hamlet A small village.

quartermaster An army officer who provides food and clothing for his troops.

rebellion An armed outbreak against authority.

regiment A military unit smaller than a brigade or division.

secede To break away.

seize To take by force.

stampede A large group that runs away in panic.

strategy A plan.

For More Information

Books

Green, Carl. *Union Generals of the Civil War* (Collective Biographies). Berkeley Heights, NJ: Enslow Publishers, 1998.

Harmon, Dan. *Civil War Generals* (Looking into the Past, People, Places, and Customs). Broomall, PA: Chelsea House, 1998.

Kent, Zachary. *William Tecumseh Sherman: Union General* (Historical American Biographies). Berkeley Heights, NJ: Enslow Publishers, 2002.

Remstein, Henna. *William Sherman: Union General* (Famous Figures of the Civil War Era). Broomall, PA: Chelsea House, 2001.

Web Sites

General William Tecumseh Sherman
www.sfmuseum.org/bio/sherman.html

A biographical web site with links to information about Sherman before and after the gold rush.

William Tecumseh Sherman: Family Papers
http://archivesl.archives.nd.edu/MSHR.HTM

This biographical web site focuses on Sherman's family life and correspondence with his wife, Ellen.

Index

William T. Sherman